TAKE TIME TO BUILD

FAITH, FAMILY, AND FINANCES

◆ ◆ ◆

by

Wanza Leftwich

Take Time to Build: Faith, Family, and Finances

Printed in the United States of America First Printing, 2024

ISBN: 979-8-9892300-3-7

Leftwich Press, Inc.
Saint Albans, NY
www.LeftwichPressChristianPublishing.com

DEDICATION

This book is dedicated to my miracle daughters, Symphony and Lyric.

After being diagnosed with infertility, God blessed me with you. He healed me and opened my womb. I love you beyond what my natural words can express.

Always remember that you can build from where you are. You are amazing, and you are loved.
-Mommy

ACKNOWLEDGMENTS

Usually, acknowledgments include names and people to thank for their love, help, and support—rightfully so. However, this time, I want to thank my husband, ***Arthur C. Leftwich, III***.

Arthur, thank you for your unwavering love and support of every hair brain scheme, plan, and business idea over the years.

Arthur, thank you for being the man you are. Through good times and bad, you've always sacrificed for your family.

Arthur, thank you for being you. I appreciate you.

Arthur, thank you for taking the time to build a life with me. I love you.

CONTENTS

TESTIMONIALS

The "Take Time to Build" movement empowers individuals and families to defeat infertility naturally, spiritually, and financially by recognizing and cultivating their God-given talents, fostering personal biblical spiritual growth and financial stability. We believe in the transformative power of faith, community, and intentional action to fulfill our God-given purpose in life. Together, we commit to breaking negative cycles, overcoming challenges, and creating a lasting impact on our families and the Kingdom of God.

Being taught by Pastor Wanza has been a wonderful experience. I came across her Facebook page in February 2022 and have been a follower since then. Open My Womb Ministries was not like any of the other groups I had joined to help guide me through my journey of infertility. The different groups were filled with inspirational quotes and women venting. Pastor Wanza's teachings are totally scripturally based, and her personal testimony is inspiring. While still on my journey to motherhood, it would be very easy to give up, but her teachings have helped me to stay positive. They have helped me to remain prayerful and keep my relationship with God at the forefront. The teachings and her genuine love for those she speaks with have also kept me hopeful in Psalm 113:19 that I WILL be a happy mother of children!

-Shalonda Davis

Richmond, Virginia

If "get you up and going" were a person, Wanza Leftwich is that person. Her gentle "No excuses" approach is what motivates movement and upward mobility in your life. While others focus on moving fast, Wanza's coaching focuses more on moving steadily, consistently, and effectively in steps, not stages. I'm convinced now, more than ever, that meeting Wanza Leftwich was a whole "God set-up" for my success.

-Dr. Cynthia McInnis

Founder, Healing Truth Women's Ministry

Author of 16 books, including HERmiletics The Workbook: HERmiletics from a Female Preacher's Perspective

One thing for sure, two things for certain: Auntie Wanza is that GWORL out in these internet streets! Especially when it comes to writing and publishing books. I hesitated to write my first book for a while, but she made me feel confident. One day, I just went for it, and before I knew it, I was done! I can attribute my confidence and completion to her dedication and never-ending encouragement. She's with you every step of the way! 10/10 highly recommend.

-Monique Heard

Fashion Stylist & Blogger

http://www.HeardShesChic.co

When it was prophesied over me, I'd write many books, I had no clue where to turn. I found out my friend's wife had a book publishing company, and I was introduced to the amazing Wanza Leftwich. She's more than a publisher; she's a coach. What I thought would be a boring, drawn-out process became an enjoyable learning experience as she and her team walked me through the process, ensuring I understood each step before moving to the next! I would never have written a book had it not been for Wanza; now I'm working on my second!

-Alfred Meyers
Author of Grief: The Silent Assassin

I will never forget my 30-minute writing consultation made easy with Wanza Leftwich. The best investment I have ever made. I paid for my consultation to help write my book and walked away with much more. That consultation manifested in my first book, An Unbreakable Bond: The Ultimate Mother and Daughter Relationship. This led to me hosting my show on Facebook, which also became my podcast, Tea Time with Tracey, T-shirt mugs, and obtaining my LLC. Wanza Leftwich back in 2018 put me on the path of Taking Time to Build. I'm in tears as I write because that one-night 30-minute consultation changed my life. It even led my daughter to write her children's book and Journal, which has put us on the road to having a legacy.
-Traccy Hines
Author of An Unbreakable Bond: The Ultimate Mother and Daughter Relationship

◆ ◆ ◆

Wanza is the best. Book her.
- Adrienne Michelle,
Executive Editor
https://iamediting.com

◆ ◆ ◆

I'm super excited to be writing again. I've had to refresh many of my technical thoughts about how publishing a book is done. One thing is sure: Wanza Leftwich is always there to fill in the blanks, keep me encouraged, and ensure my books are ready for

publishing. I don't know about your publisher, but Wanza is ALWAYS available and ready to jump right in and help me meet that deadline and publish my thoughts.
-Dr. Monique Porter
Author multiple books, including Jail Dad

Wanza encouraged me to put my poems into a book. That idea never crossed my mind. Wanza is a seed planter. She helped me publish my first book of poetry, It's Time for You to Soar, and my second book, Wounded Worshipper. Her expertise in book publishing is second to none. She is efficient, professional, and knowledgeable. I highly recommend using her service. You will be pleased as I was.
-Tarinna Olley
Founder of Jesus & Therapy, Too
http://www.TarinnaOlley.com

Working with Wanza was impactful. I don't consider myself a writer by any means. My preference for communication primarily is speaking. However, after working with Wanza, I completed my third devotional. I completed my first devotional a week after applying her coaching. I've followed the model she teaches ever since. Her easy system for writing is perfect for those who desire to articulate their thoughts to the world with ease. Her practical teaching style will enable you to begin birthing your books almost effortlessly. She has truly taught me how to put my pen to the pad stress-free.
-Saquoye J. Tarver
Author of I Choose Life Series

INTRODUCTION

Have you ever felt loyal at church but broken at home, dedicated at work but struggling in your personal life, or a successful entrepreneur constantly facing failed relationships? You must take time to build in the areas where you fall short.

I realized this a few years ago when God spoke to me. At that time, I was distraught and angry. I was frustrated because I believed I was doing all the right things. I was faithful and loyal, yet my house was in disarray. My soul felt empty. I was living in debt, far beyond my means. I kept asking God, "Why don't I have enough? Why can't I pay the bills? Why must I choose between paying bills and providing for my child? I've been sowing seeds faithfully, so where is the blessing?"

Seeing my girls grow up made me realize even more that I hadn't given attention to building something of my own. It was eye-opening to recognize that, despite all my efforts, I had nothing physical to leave them. Being this busy, helpful, faithful, and still unable to provide for them or leave them something was a harsh reality. I knew I had to change that.

God showed me myself. On one side, I was loyal and faithful; the church couldn't open without me. I was at every service, serving diligently. But at home, everything was neglected. The house was unclean, the bills were unpaid, and nothing was organized. I was highly efficient in one part of my life but chaotic in another.

Seven days after having my first baby, I was back in church. Two days later, I was back at work. People thought I was crazy. I thought I was crazy. More than that, I was scared and broke with a baby. God had answered my prayers! I had a baby when the doctors said I was infertile. I should have been rejoicing, sleeping, and cuddling my new baby. But I was back at work because we were in so much debt, living far beyond paycheck to paycheck.

Can I be honest? I just knew that wouldn't last long—until it did. Being broke, scared, and saved lasted another ten-plus years. We even had another baby. Don't get me wrong—I was grateful, and every day wasn't bad.

However, one day, I realized I wasn't doing all that God wanted me to do. I needed to take time to build. God spoke to my heart, saying, "Wanza, you must take time to build." This revelation hit me hard. I realized I had been building for others—helping people develop their ministries, encouraging them—but I had neglected to build anything for myself. I remember sitting in my car, crying uncontrollably, feeling like I had to start over after all these years. It felt like my work was in vain.

Writing this now brings tears to my eyes. It was devastating to hear God tell me I had to build. I felt lost and deceived as if all my years of service and sacrifice amounted to nothing. I had to face the fact that I had neglected my family, one of the most significant areas of my life. Understanding this truth was incredibly painful. I had so much to rebuild—bills to pay, relationships to mend, and personal dreams to pursue.

Would I ever reach the dreams I held in my heart? Would I ever become the person I envisioned? The journey was painful, but it was essential. I had rushed through life, pleasing others and neglecting myself, believing it was for the kingdom. Yet, if I cared for myself, I realized I could better serve the kingdom.

Let that sink in: If you care for yourself, your business, and your family, you can serve the kingdom far better than you are now.

Prayer

Heavenly Father,

I come before You with a humble heart, recognizing the areas where I have fallen short. I have neglected to build the foundations you called me to establish. Lord, I seek Your guidance and strength as I embark on this journey of rebuilding. Help me prioritize my family, home, and myself to serve Your kingdom better.

Thank You for the blessings You have given me and for the revelation that I need to take time to build. Grant me the wisdom to make the right choices, the patience to endure the process, and the faith to trust in Your plans. May I be diligent in my efforts and faithful in my obedience to You?

In Jesus' name, I pray. Amen.

Confession

I confess that I have often neglected my well-being and my family's needs while striving to serve others. I have been so focused on being faithful and loyal outside my home that I failed to take care of what truly matters within it. I admit my mistakes, repent, and ask for your forgiveness.

I declare that I am now committed to taking time to build in the areas where I have been lacking. I will prioritize my family, my finances, and my personal growth. I will seek God's guidance daily and trust His plans for my life. I can serve the kingdom more effectively by caring for myself and my family.

Track & Reflect

Complete the Introduction in the Take Time to Build Companion Guide and Tracker

CHAPTER ONE: LET'S PRAY

"Start this book off with prayer."

"God, isn't this a *build your life-personal growth type* of book?"

"Yes."

Why start this book with prayer, God? Prayer is essential communication with God, who is able and willing to direct you in all things. What sticks out to me is the "willing" part. Often, we stay in what I like to call "struggleville" too long because we refuse to ask God for His help.

When Daniel asked God about the king's troubling dream, God answered him.

"Then Daniel went in and desired of the king that he would give him time and that he would shew the king the interpretation. Then was the secret revealed unto Daniel in a night vision. Then Daniel blessed the God of heaven. Daniel answered and said, Blessed be the name of God for ever and ever: for wisdom and might are his: And he changeth the times and the seasons: he removeth kings, and setteth up kings: he giveth wisdom unto the wise, and knowledge to them that know understanding: He revealeth the deep and secret things: he knoweth what is in the darkness, and the light dwelleth with him. I thank thee, and praise thee, O thou God of my fathers, who hast given me wisdom and might, and hast made known unto me now what we desired of thee: for thou hast now made known unto us the king's matter." (Daniel 2:16-23)

When David inquired of the Lord, God gave him an answer.

"And it came to pass after this, that David enquired of the Lord, saying, Shall I go up into any of the cities of Judah? And the Lord said unto him, Go up. And David said, Whither shall I go up? And he said, Unto Hebron." (2 Samuel 2:1)

When Joshua prayed, God gave him an answer.

"And the Lord said unto Joshua, Get thee up; wherefore liest thou thus upon thy face? Israel hath sinned, and they have also transgressed my covenant which I commanded them: for they have even taken of the accursed thing, and have also stolen, and dissembled also, and they have put it even among their own stuff. Therefore the children of Israel could not stand before their enemies, but turned their backs on their enemies, because they were accursed: neither will I be with you any more, except ye destroy the accursed from among you. Up, sanctify the people, and say, Sanctify yourselves against to morrow: for thus saith the Lord God of Israel, There is an accursed thing in the midst of thee, O Israel: thou canst not stand before thine enemies, until ye take away the accursed thing from among you." (Joshua 7:10-13)

When you pray, God will give you an answer.

Prayer is essential to the believer's life and building your life. It is our direct line of communication with God. Through prayer, we receive direction, wisdom, and strategies to navigate the complexities of life and business. Proverbs 3:5- 6 (KJV) reminds us to "Trust in the Lord with all thine heart; and lean not unto thine own understanding. In all thy ways acknowledge him, and he shall direct thy paths."

When we make prayer a priority, we invite God into our situations. We open the door for divine insight and solutions beyond human wisdom. Whether making a crucial business decision, resolving a conflict, or seeking new opportunities, prayer positions us to receive God's best. Remember, God is not only able but willing to guide us. As it is written in James 1:5 (KJV), "If any of you lack wisdom, let him ask of God, that giveth to all men liberally, and upbraideth not; and it shall be given him."

Starting this book with prayer declares that we invite God to be an integral part of our business journey. It is a testament to our belief that we can achieve the extraordinary with God's guidance. So, let us pray:

"Heavenly Father, we thank You for this opportunity to take time to build my faith, family, and finances with You. I acknowledge Your wisdom, power, and willingness to help me. I ask for Your guidance, insight, and strategies. Lead me in the way I should go, and help me to trust in Your plans for my life.

In Jesus' name, we pray. Amen."

Courageous Confessions

1. **I commit my plans to the Lord, and He will establish my steps.**
   "Commit thy works unto the Lord, and thy thoughts shall be established." (Proverbs 16:3)

2. **I am confident that God hears my prayers and answers them.**
   "And this is the confidence that we have in him, that, if we ask any thing according to his will, he heareth us." (1 John 5:14)

3. **I renew my mind daily through prayer and scripture.**
   "And be not conformed to this world: but be ye transformed by the renewing of your mind..." (Romans 12:2)

4. I walk by faith, knowing God is directing my path.

"For we walk by faith, not by sight." (2 Corinthians 5:7)

5. I trust in the Lord with all my heart and lean not on my own understanding.

"Trust in the Lord with all thine heart; and lean not unto thine own understanding." (Proverbs 3:5)

6. My prayers are powerful and effective, accomplishing God's will.

"The effectual fervent prayer of a righteous man availeth much." (James 5:16)

7. I surrender my worries to God, for He cares for me.

"Casting all your care upon him; for he careth for you." (1 Peter 5:7)

8. I seek God's guidance in every decision I make.

"In all thy ways acknowledge him, and he shall direct thy paths." (Proverbs 3:6)

9. I am at peace knowing God is in my life.

"And the peace of God, which passeth all understanding, shall keep your hearts and minds through Christ Jesus." (Philippians 4:7)

10. Through prayer, I find strength and courage for every challenge.

"I can do all things through Christ which strengtheneth me." (Philippians 4:13)

Track & Reflect

Scan and Receive 31 Days of Courageous Confessions

Complete Let's Pray in your Take Time to Build Companion Guide & Tracker

CHAPTER TWO: PERMISSION TO BUILD

Can we chat? Great. Let me tell you about two days that changed my life forever.

Day One

I was at church but needed to visit the nearby beauty supply store. My heart was so heavy as I entered the store. I got what I needed and returned to my car. By the time I got to my car, I was in tears. Ask me why. I'm glad you asked...

I was tired, frustrated, and fed up with everything. "God, how come this isn't working like you said?" "Why am I faithful and broke?" "I'm always working with nothing to show for it." "God, what is going on?"

I cried and cried and heard, "You have to take time to build." "Lord, I've been building for years!" "You have to take time to build you..."

I thought I was hearing incorrectly. Say what? What do you mean? "You've neglected your house. You're building here and there, but not at home." "God, my faithfulness here doesn't 'transfer' over there?"

Well, baby, I thought I had been hoodwinked, run amok, bamboozled, and outright punked. What is happening? What do you mean? I've been building, and I'm tired. What more could I possibly do?

God began to show me. Listen to me: I cried so hard in that car because I just knew I was doing the right thing, and God showed me how much more I needed to do. And to be quite honest, I didn't know if I could do what He said.

This day marked the beginning of a significant change in my life. It was no longer about anyone else but about me. Often, you may ask yourself, what is going on? What's the issue or problem? Why am I facing so many difficulties in my life?

I asked God, "What's wrong with me?" There's nothing wrong with you. However, the way you're doing things may be incorrect for you. I thought I was right. I thought my faithfulness at church and to others would help me out. Don't get me wrong, these things have their place, but being faithful doesn't translate into your bills being paid unless you're a faithful steward over your finances. Oh, I run the risk of exposing my former thought process, but who would that help? No one.

Your thoughts turn into actions, and your actions become your life. My thinking was off and out of alignment with God's word. My thoughts made me feel good. I thought I was doing well. I thought I was being faithful. I thought this was what God wanted. I thought this was what so and so wanted. But what was God thinking? What were His plans for my life?

When God revealed to me that to have what I was praying for, I needed to change what I was doing. Did God say to become unfaithful at church? He did not. He said to become faithful in the area in which I was lacking. See, when you ignore the problem, try to pray it away, and tell God to handle it… It doesn't work like that.

The things that you can do, you must do.

If you want a new car, fix your credit. If you want a new job, apply for it. If you want a spouse, prepare for them.

See where I'm going? You can't make God responsible for your part of the relationship. God will do what He does, but He can't do your part. He can't make you pay your bills on time. He can't make you forgive your loved one. He can't make you, and you can't make Him. This is a mutually beneficial relationship that is governed by kingdom principles.

Day Two

The phone rang while driving down Atlantic Avenue in Brooklyn, NY. If you know anything about Brooklyn, you know that your driving skills should be up to par, and the fewer distractions while driving, the better. I usually don't answer phone numbers I don't know, and you probably don't either. But that day, I did, and somehow, I already knew it wasn't good news. God has a way of preparing you in a moment.

I answered the phone, and to my heartbreak, the job offer I recently received was rescinded. Gone. Just like that. I don't remember the exact words, but I remember an immediate shift in my thinking. Once again, I was an overly qualified person without a job. In an effort to "humble" myself and be "willing to start from the bottom," I agreed to take a position nearly an hour away from home with NYC traffic during rush hour. I changed my daughters' schools to accommodate the new work schedule so they could be closer to me. I had begun changing my life because of this job offer, and it was quickly taken away with a two-minute phone call.

At that very moment, I wanted to cry in my car on Atlantic Ave. I don't remember if I cried, but I recall that shift. The one that changed everything for me and my family. The shift that said, "I'm not taking another job. I'm going to do what I believe You want me to do. I'll homeschool my girls and work my business."

I was scared—yes, I admit it—but I was determined to try. Could God be right? Could I homeschool my girls and build a successful business? Was it possible to live off my husband's salary while doing so? As you can imagine, I do not like being broke or having unpaid bills. However, that never stopped me from being broke or late with bills before.

Could God be right? Could I do this? Be that homeschool mom I always wanted to be? Be that media mogul and business strategist with happy clients who paid me well? Amid my grief over losing a job, I never got a chance to start; I had many questions for God about the "how," but certainly not the "why" of the next move I would make. I didn't see my bills getting paid. I didn't see anyone understanding why I would homeschool my girls. I didn't see much, but I knew that if I didn't take the time to build what God wanted, I would regret it for the rest of my life.

So, on that long ride down Atlantic Ave, heading toward home, I decided to live a life of quality over a life of practical and traditional work-life roles and raising children. Little did I know that in less than two years, we would experience a global pandemic that would forever change how we work and how our children learn.

Between these two days, God impressed upon me to build a life that glorified Him at the expense of my thinking and comfort. He is giving you that opportunity as well. His permission to build your family and business through kingdom principles is all you need. His direction is wiser than any guru, expert, coach, or therapist you can hire to direct you. Yes, they all have their place. However, do not suspect God's instructions on your journey. His ways are not our ways; neither are His thoughts. He knows how to direct you to bring you out of "struggleville" in your faith, family, and business.

Courageous Confessions

1. I embrace the journey of building my life with God's purpose.

"Being confident of this very thing, that he which hath begun a good work in you will perform it until the day of Jesus Christ." (Philippians 1:6)

2. I am not afraid to step out of my comfort zone to follow God's plan.

"Fear thou not; for I am with thee: be not dismayed; for I am thy God." (Isaiah 41:10)

3. I trust that God is equipping me for the work ahead.

"And he gave some, apostles; and some, prophets; and some, evangelists; and some, pastors and teachers." (Ephesians 4:12)

4. I choose quality over convenience in my life decisions.

"And whatsoever ye do, do it heartily, as to the Lord, and not unto men." (Colossians 3:23)

5. I acknowledge my fears and choose to act in faith.

"For God hath not given us the spirit of fear; but of power, and of love, and of a sound mind." (2 Timothy 1:7)

6. I am committed to building my family and business according to God's principles.

"Therefore whosoever heareth these sayings of mine, and doeth them, I will liken him unto a wise man, which built his house upon a rock." (Matthew 7:24)

7. I will not allow setbacks to deter me from my purpose.

"And we know that all things work together for good to them that love God..." (Romans 8:28)

8. I am determined to homeschool my children and nurture their growth.
"Train up a child in the way he should go: and when he is old, he will not depart from it." (Proverbs 22:6)

9. I believe God has a more excellent plan for my life than I can imagine.
"For I know the thoughts that I think toward you, saith the Lord, thoughts of peace, and not of evil, to give you an expected end." (Jeremiah 29:11)

10. I will take time to build what God has placed in my heart.
"Then answered I them, and said unto them, The God of heaven, he will prosper us; therefore we his servants will arise and build." (Nehemiah 2:20)

Track & Reflect

Watch – Scan QR Code
Why You Should Take Time to Build

Complete Permission to Build in your Take Time to Build Companion Guide & Tracker

CHAPTER THREE: THE "A" WORD

This girl has done everything from writing resumes to creating souvenirs and keepsakes for special events. I've tried several things over the years, including multiple multi-level marketing businesses (which I love). You can say business is in me. I had that entrepreneurial bug for years, always doing something, always a side hustle, always advising others on how to make an extra dollar.

The funny thing is, I rarely took my advice. I helped others achieve their goals, yet I had not done the same. Ironic, huh? It is possible to help build others and not reach your own goals.

It's structured into our lives to be responsible and build others before we do it for ourselves. In ministry, it is structured as primary and secondary leadership duties and roles. Now stay with me. The way God deals with me is different, and I have entirely accepted this as I took time to build over the last few years.

In the context of church organization or corporate structure, an example of primary leadership is the CEO or Pastor. A secondary leader is the Director, Assistant Pastor, or higher leadership role in either entity. The primary leader gives the instruction or has the vision for the entire organization. The secondary leader carries out the instruction or vision according to the primary leader's wishes. My experience has been that when you are consistently in a secondary leadership role at work or church, this can translate to secondary leadership in your own life. What does that mean, Wanza?

It means that because you are used to following instructions, you have put aside the fact that you are the primary leader in your life. Does that make sense? I'm not saying, "Don't follow your leader or boss." I would never say that because we are to do what is right. I am saying that you can forget that you are responsible for your own life and actions outside the church or a corporate structure.

Wanza, what does this look like? It looks like you are doing a great job as an accountant but cannot pay your bills at home. It looks like submitting to your pastor's words but arguing with your spouse about their simple requests. You follow quickly as a secondary leader; however, you cannot take a secondary role in your personal lives at home and in your own business. You are the primary leader. The responsibility for success is on you. You have to become accountable for your life.

Taking personal accountability for the outcome (good or bad) is the difference between primary and secondary leaders. You remain as secondary leaders in your own life because you don't want to take accountability for the outcome. Now, what does that look like? I can't cook tonight because I have Bible Study. I can get a promotion at work but can't return to school because I don't have the money. Primary leaders are accountable to their vision and figure out a solution to their problem or circumstance because they know the desired outcome they want, and they will accept nothing less than that.

Are you ready to be accountable to God's plans for your life? What plans does God have for you? What have you suppressed because you're in second place in your life?

The value of your life is measured by God and not by you. He decided that you would be born. In **Jeremiah 1:5 (KJV)**, God declares, "Before I formed thee in the belly I knew thee; and before thou camest forth out of the womb I sanctified thee, and I ordained thee a prophet unto the nations." This verse illustrates that God has a specific plan and purpose for us even before birth. Jeremiah's life had immense value in God's eyes, and so does yours.

Consider these scriptures that demonstrate God's value for our lives and His plans for us:

1. **Psalm 139:13-14 (KJV)**: "For thou hast possessed my reins: thou hast covered me in my mother's womb. I will praise thee; for I am fearfully and wonderfully made: marvellous are thy works; and that my soul knoweth right well." God's intricate design of each person shows His value and care for us.
2. **Ephesians 2:10 (KJV)**: "For we are his workmanship, created in Christ Jesus unto good works, which God hath before ordained that we should walk in them." God has prepared good works for us to do, demonstrating His plans for our lives.
3. **Isaiah 49:1 (KJV)**: "Listen, O isles, unto me; and hearken, ye people, from far; The LORD hath called me from the womb; from the bowels of my mother hath he made mention of my name." God's calling on our lives is from the very beginning.

Taking personal accountability means recognizing and stepping into the plans that God has for you. It's understanding that while you may be a secondary leader at work or church, you are the primary leader in your own life. You must take the initiative to follow God's instructions and fulfill His purpose for you. This requires diligence, faithfulness, and a willingness to step out of your comfort zone.

The scripture in **1 Timothy 5:8 (KJV)** is a sobering reminder: "But if any provide not for his own, and specially for those of his own house, he hath denied the faith, and is worse than an infidel." This emphasizes the importance of taking responsibility for our households. We are called to be stewards of our families and homes, ensuring their needs are met and leading them according to God's principles.

Are you ready to be accountable for God's plans for your life? Embrace the role of primary leader in your own life and take the necessary steps to fulfill God's calling. Trust in His guidance, for His plans are always for the good and His glory.

Courageous Confessions

1. **I take full accountability for my life and choices.**

"For every man shall bear his burden." (Galatians 6:5)

2. **I am a primary leader in my own life, responsible for my future.**

"Moreover, it is required in stewards, that a man be found faithful." (1 Corinthians 4:2)

3. **I commit to nurturing my home and family with love and care.**

"But if any provide not for his own, and specially for those of his own house, he hath denied the faith, and is worse than an infidel." (1 Timothy 5:8)

4. **I am not afraid to take the lead in pursuing my dreams.**

"A man's heart deviseth his way: but the Lord directeth his steps." (Proverbs 16:9)

5. **I will no longer suppress my goals or aspirations.**

"I press toward the mark for the prize of the high calling of God in Christ Jesus." (Philippians 3:14)

6. I choose to act upon God's calling for my life with courage.

"Have not I commanded thee? Be strong and of a good courage; be not afraid, neither be thou dismayed." (Joshua 1:9)

7. I am determined to build a legacy that honors God and my family.

"A good man leaveth an inheritance to his children's children." (Proverbs 13:22)

8. I will invest in my personal growth and development.

"But grow in grace, and in the knowledge of our Lord and Saviour Jesus Christ." (2 Peter 3:18)

9. I am a faithful steward of the resources and responsibilities God has given me.

"He that is faithful in that which is least is faithful also in much." (Luke 16:10)

10. I believe in my God-given value and His plans for me.

"Before I formed thee in the belly I knew thee; and before thou camest forth out of the womb I sanctified thee." (Jeremiah 1:5)

Track & Reflect

Complete The "A" Word in your Take Time to Build Companion Guide & Tracker

CHAPTER FOUR: THE DISCOVERY

One day, I discovered that you can be faithful and broke, faithful and weary, and faithful and disobedient to God.

That day, I cried and cried. I discovered that I was faithful but broke, and I did not want to die that way. One of my favorite passages in the Bible is II Kings 4. The widow is my hero. She is my poster person for creating a business out of nothing, rescuing her children from bondage by paying off her debt and living off the rest. She is the woman.

But before we continue to celebrate her, let's look at the entire passage. What caused her to start this business to save her family?

In II Kings 4:1-7, we read about a woman whose husband had died and left her in debt. Her husband was a faithful servant of God, yet he left his family in dire straits. This was not a reputable thing to do, leaving his wife desperate and vulnerable.

"Now there cried a certain woman of the wives of the sons of the prophets unto Elisha, saying, Thy servant my husband is dead; and thou knowest that thy servant did fear the Lord: and the creditor is come to take unto him my two sons to be bondmen." (II Kings 4:1)

The prophet Elisha did not pity her but gave her a solution. He asked her what she had in her house.

"And Elisha said unto her, What shall I do for thee? tell me, what hast

thou in the house? And she said, Thine handmaid hath not any thing in the house, save a pot of oil." (II Kings 4:2)

He instructed her to borrow empty vessels from her neighbors, not a few, and to pour out the oil she had into all those vessels.

"Then he said, Go, borrow thee vessels abroad of all thy neighbours, even empty vessels; borrow not a few. And when thou art come in, thou shalt shut the door upon thee and upon thy sons, and shalt pour out into all those vessels, and thou shalt set aside that which is full." (II Kings 4:3-4)

She obeyed and filled all the vessels. When there were no more vessels to fill, the oil stopped flowing.

"So she went from him, and shut the door upon her and upon her sons, who brought the vessels to her; and she poured out. And it came to pass, when the vessels were full, that she said unto her son, Bring me yet a vessel. And he said unto her, There is not a vessel more. And the oil stayed." (II Kings 4:5-6)

Elisha told her to sell the oil, pay her debt, and live off the rest.

"Then she came and told the man of God. And he said, Go, sell the oil, and pay thy debt, and live thou and thy children of the rest." (II Kings 4:7)

The widow's husband had access to the same prophet but did not have a solution for his family. He was a faithful servant, leaving his family in a precarious situation. How could this be? Faithfulness does not always equate to wisdom in managing one's household.

The Bible tells us that we must take care of our household. Let's review this passage of scripture again.

"But if any provide not for his own, and specially for those of his own house, he hath denied the faith, and is worse than an infidel." (1

Timothy 5:8)

This scripture emphasizes the importance of taking responsibility for our families. The widow's husband failed in this aspect, leaving his wife to deal with the consequences.

This passage challenges us to reflect on our own lives. Are we being faithful yet neglecting our responsibilities? Are we relying solely on faithfulness without seeking God's wisdom and guidance in managing our households and resources?

The prophet Elisha's solution to the widow's problem teaches us that God provides us with resources to use. It is not enough to be faithful; we must also be diligent and resourceful. God's provision often comes with instructions that require our active participation.

The widow of II Kings 4 is a powerful example of faith in action. She did not sit idly by, waiting for a miracle. She sought help, obeyed the prophet's instructions, and used what she had to secure her family's future.

Her story inspires us to be proactive, seek God's guidance in every area of our lives, and take responsibility for the well-being of our families. We must be faithful and wise stewards of the resources God has given us, ensuring that we do not leave our loved ones vulnerable.

What resources has God given you that you need to utilize more effectively? How can you ensure you are faithful and wise in managing your household and resources?

Courageous Confessions

1. I am a wise and faithful steward of the resources God has given me.

"Moreover it is required in stewards, that a man be found faithful." (1 Corinthians 4:2)

2. I take responsibility for the well-being of my household, ensuring we are provided for.

"But if any provide not for his own, and specially for those of his own house, he hath denied the faith, and is worse than an infidel." (1 Timothy 5:8)

3. I trust God to provide solutions for every challenge I face, just as He did for the widow.

"The LORD is my shepherd; I shall not want." (Psalm 23:1)

4. I actively participate in God's plans, wisely using the resources He has given me.

"Whatsoever thy hand findeth to do, do it with thy might." (Ecclesiastes 9:10)

5. I seek God's guidance in managing my household and resources.

"Trust in the LORD with all thine heart; and lean not unto thine own understanding. In all thy ways acknowledge him, and he shall direct thy paths." (Proverbs 3:5-6)

6. I am proactive and diligent, ensuring my family's needs are met through God's provision.

"The hand of the diligent shall bear rule: but the slothful shall be under tribute." (Proverbs 12:24)

7. I do not rely solely on my own understanding but seek God's wisdom in all things.

"If any of you lack wisdom, let him ask of God, that giveth to all men liberally, and upbraideth not; and it shall be given him." (James 1:5)

8. I am faithful in small things, knowing God will entrust me with greater responsibilities.

"He that is faithful in that which is least is faithful also in much: and he that is unjust in the least is unjust also in much." (Luke 16:10)

9. I honor God in my finances, ensuring my family is not left in debt or need.

"Owe no man any thing, but to love one another: for he that loveth another hath fulfilled the law." (Romans 13:8)

10. God empowers me to create solutions and meet my family's needs.

"But thou shalt remember the LORD thy God: for it is he that giveth thee power to get wealth, that he may establish his covenant which he sware unto thy fathers, as it is this day." (Deuteronomy 8:18)

Track & Reflect
Scan and Watch: One Skill to Debt Freedom

Complete The Discovery in your Take Time to Build Companion Guide & Tracker

CHAPTER FIVE: SHUT THE DOOR

One pot of oil changed the trajectory of the widow's and her children's lives. She was able to pay off her debt and live off the rest. Think about that for a moment. What resource or "one thing" have you been neglecting?

Building your family and finances doesn't take ten skills or talents. You can make it with one. God can increase what you recognize and use. She obeyed the instructions—no pretense, questions asked, or doubts if it would work. She revered the words of the prophet and took action.

She shut the door and obeyed the prophet. The prophet didn't ask her to work with anyone else. It was her and her family.

Family Unity and Obedience

In 2 Kings 4:4, we read, "And when thou art come in, thou shalt shut the door upon thee and upon thy sons, and shalt pour out into all those vessels, and thou shalt set aside that which is full."

The widow involved her family in the miracle. She and her sons shut the door, symbolizing a private act of faith and obedience. This act shows the importance of family unity and working together toward a common goal. Each member had a role to play, and together, they witnessed God's provision.

Working Together in Faith

Imagine the scene: the widow pouring oil into the vessels while her sons brought her empty ones. They all witnessed the miracle unfold. They were in it together, supporting one another and obeying God's directive through the prophet Elisha. This unity and collective faith are essential for families today. When we work together and follow God's instructions, we, too, can experience His miraculous provision.

In 2 Kings 4:5-6, the Bible says, "So she went from him, and shut the door upon her and her sons, who brought the vessels to her; and she poured out. And it came to pass, when the vessels were full, that she said unto her son, Bring me yet a vessel. And he said unto her, There is not a vessel more. And the oil stayed."

The Power of Obedience

The widow's story teaches us the power of obedience. She didn't hesitate or question the prophet's instructions. Her obedience and her sons' help led to a miraculous provision that saved her family from bondage. Shutting the door signifies focusing on God's promise and blocking distractions or doubts.

God can multiply whatever you have if you bring it to Him in faith. The widow's story is a powerful reminder that God's provision often comes through our obedience and collaboration with those closest to us.

When you unite, especially within your families, you create an environment where God's blessings flow freely. Trust in God's plan, involve your family and watch as He works and wonders through your collective faith and obedience.

Courageous Confessions

1. **I believe God can use my little to bless me abundantly.**

"And when thou art come in, thou shalt shut the door upon thee and upon thy sons, and shalt pour out into all those vessels, and thou shalt set aside that which is full." (2 Kings 4:4)

2. I will shut the door on doubt and distractions, focusing solely on God's promises.
"So she went from him, and shut the door upon her and upon her sons, who brought the vessels to her; and she poured out." (2 Kings 4:5)

3. I trust in God's provision and will involve my family in His plans for us.
"Behold, how good and how pleasant it is for brethren to dwell together in unity!" (Psalm 133:1)

4. I am obedient to God's instructions, knowing He will provide for all my needs.
"And it came to pass, when the vessels were full, that she said unto her son, Bring me yet a vessel. And he said unto her, There is not a vessel more. And the oil stayed." (2 Kings 4:6)

5. God multiplies my resources when I bring them to Him in faith.
"Give, and it shall be given unto you; good measure, pressed down, and shaken together, and running over, shall men give into your bosom." (Luke 6:38)

6. My family and I will work together to fulfill God's plans for us.
"Behold, how good and how pleasant it is for brethren to dwell together in unity!" (Psalm 133:1)

7. God has a plan for me and my family, and we will walk

according to His word.

"For I know the thoughts that I think toward you, saith the Lord, thoughts of peace, and not of evil, to give you an expected end." (Jeremiah 29:11)

8. I will not let fear or uncertainty hinder me from following God's instructions.

"For God hath not given us the spirit of fear; but of power, and of love, and of a sound mind." (2 Timothy 1:7)

9. I trust that God will turn my little into much when I follow His guidance.

"And Jesus took the loaves; and when he had given thanks, he distributed to the disciples, and the disciples to them that were set down; and likewise of the fishes as much as they would." (John 6:11)

10. I believe God will provide for me and my family as we walk in His ways.

"But my God shall supply all your need according to his riches in glory by Christ Jesus." (Philippians 4:19)

Track & Reflect
Scan and Watch

Use What You Have to Get Out of Debt

Complete Shut the Door in your Take Time to Build Companion Guide & Tracker

CHAPTER SIX: DOING WHAT I'VE NEVER DONE

Building inner emotional capacity is essential when doing something you've never done before. We all face distractions and emotional challenges that can easily set us back. Recognizing negative patterns and cycles is crucial to breaking free and moving toward our goals.

Staying Focused

Staying focused is a choice we make daily. Distractions can come in many forms—self-doubt, fear of failure, or even the opinions of others. Just like the Israelites, who wandered in the desert for forty years due to their inability to trust God's promises, we can allow our emotional struggles to hold us back. As it says in **Hebrews 12:1**, "Wherefore seeing we also are compassed about with so great a cloud of witnesses, let us lay aside every weight, and the sin which doth so easily beset us, and let us run with patience the race that is set before us."

Emotional Distractions

Identifying and confronting the emotional distractions that impede our progress is essential. Here are some common emotional distractions:

1. **Grief**: The widow woman could have been overwhelmed by her loss, but instead, she chose to take action to save her sons and her family's future.

2. **Fear**: Fear of failure can paralyze us, making us hesitant to step out of our comfort zones.
3. **Self-Doubt**: Questioning our abilities can prevent us from pursuing our dreams.
4. **Anxiety**: Worrying about the future can prevent us from focusing on the present.
5. **Regret**: Dwelling on past mistakes can distract us from moving forward.
6. **Comparison**: Comparing ourselves to others can lead to feelings of inadequacy and stagnation.
7. **Overwhelm**: Feeling overloaded by responsibilities can cause us to freeze instead of taking action.
8. **Procrastination**: Putting things off due to fear or uncertainty can create cycles of inaction.
9. **Negative Relationships**: Toxic relationships can drain our energy and focus, pulling us away from our goals.
10. **Distractions from the World**: Social media, news, and daily life noise can divert our attention from what truly matters.

Leaving the Cycle Behind

To improve our lives, we must be willing to leave behind what no longer serves us. Consider Gideon, who God called to save Israel from the Midianites. Initially, Gideon felt unqualified and overwhelmed, saying, "Oh my Lord, wherewith shall I save Israel? Behold, my family is poor in Manasseh, and I am the least in my father's house" (Judges 6:15). Yet, despite his fears, Gideon chose to obey God's call, demonstrating that our feelings of inadequacy do not define our potential.

Similarly, David is just a shepherd boy when he faces Goliath. Despite his youth and inexperience in battle, he stepped up to challenge the giant, declaring, "Thou comest to me with a sword, and with a spear, and with a shield: but I come to thee in the name of the Lord of hosts" (1 Samuel 17:45). David's faith and courage transformed his destiny, proving that stepping out of our comfort zones leads to great victories.

Embrace Your Skills

You don't need to invent something new to achieve your dreams. Often, the skills you already possess are more than enough. Just look at the disciples—they were fishermen. When they needed money to pay the temple tax, Jesus instructed Peter to catch a fish, and inside its mouth was a coin. As it says in **Matthew 17:27**, "Notwithstanding, lest we should offend them, go thou to the sea, and cast an hook, and take up the fish that first cometh up; and when thou hast opened his mouth, thou shalt find a piece of money." This miracle shows us that sometimes the answer to our problems lies within the very skills we already have.

Recognizing Patterns

Like Jesus, who faced distractions yet remained focused on His mission, we, too, must identify the emotional distractions that keep us from fulfilling our purpose. Jesus was constantly pursued by crowds and faced opposition, but He stayed the course and focused on His calling. In **Luke 9:51**, it says, "And it came to pass, when the time was come that he should be received up, he stedfastly set his face to go to Jerusalem." His determination inspires us to do the same.

The widow could have succumbed to her grief and allowed her life to fall apart, but instead, she took action. She asked questions, sought answers, and began to build a new future for herself and her sons. Just like her, you cannot let life's challenges paralyze you. You must take steps forward, even if they are small ones. The power to change your life lies within you. Embrace your skills, recognize the emotional distractions, and choose to break the negative cycles. Like Gideon and David, you can do what you've never done!

Courageous Confessions

1.I am building my inner emotional capacity to achieve new heights.

"I can do all things through Christ which strengtheneth me." - Philippians 4:13

2. I stay focused and overcome emotional distractions with God's help.

"Set your affection on things above, not on things on the earth." - Colossians 3:2

3. I recognize and break negative patterns and cycles in my life.

"And be not conformed to this world: but be ye transformed by the renewing of your mind, that ye may prove what is that good, and acceptable, and perfect, will of God." - Romans 12:2

4. I am equipped to leave behind any cycle that hinders my progress.

"Wherefore seeing we also are compassed about with so great a cloud of witnesses, let us lay aside every weight, and the sin which doth so easily beset us, and let us run with patience the race that is set before us." - Hebrews 12:1

5. I use the skills God has given me to build a better life.

"As every man hath received the gift, even so minister the same one to another, as good stewards of the manifold grace of God." - 1 Peter 4:10

6. I am not afraid to do what I've never done before, trusting in God's guidance.

"Have not I commanded thee? Be strong and of a good courage; be not afraid, neither be thou dismayed: for the Lord thy God is with thee whithersoever thou goest." - Joshua 1:9

7. I believe that God increases what I have when I act in faith.

"But my God shall supply all your need according to his riches in glory by Christ Jesus." - Philippians 4:19

8. I am committed to breaking free from emotional distractions and staying focused on God's plan.

"Casting down imaginations, and every high thing that exalteth itself against the knowledge of God, and bringing into captivity every thought to the obedience of Christ." - 2 Corinthians 10:5

9. I trust in God's plan for my life, even when it requires me to step out of my comfort zone.

"Trust in the Lord with all thine heart; and lean not unto thine own understanding. In all thy ways acknowledge him, and he shall direct thy paths." - Proverbs 3:5-6

10. I embrace the unique path God has set for me, knowing He equips me for every challenge.

"Being confident of this very thing, that he which hath begun a good work in you will perform it until the day of Jesus Christ." - Philippians 1:6

Track & Reflect

Complete Doing What I've Never Done in your Take Time to Build

Companion Guide & Tracker

CHAPTER SEVEN: INCREASE MY MONEY

Have you ever heard that you can turn your talent into profit? Well, you can, and it's not a cliché. It's truly a God-given gift to make money and provide for yourself and your family from what's within you. It's easy to overlook and neglect what comes naturally. You often fail to see its value because you're a natural. However, recognizing and utilizing your gifts is crucial for your progress in personal life, family well-being, and ability to contribute to the Kingdom of God.

God's Desire for Your Financial Increase

God desires for us to thrive, not just survive. He has provided each of us with unique talents and resources that, when utilized correctly, can lead to significant financial growth. One profound example is found in **Matthew 25:14-30**, the Parable of the Talents, where Jesus illustrates the importance of using what we've been given:

"For the kingdom of heaven is as a man traveling into a far country, who called his own servants, and delivered unto them his goods." (Matthew 25:14)

In this parable, the servants were entrusted with different amounts of talents. The ones who actively invested and utilized what they were given saw an increase, while the ones who hid their talents faced the consequences. This teaches us that God expects us to put our gifts to work.

Examples of Financial Increase

1. **The Widow's Oil**
   The widow in **2 Kings 4:1-7** had only a small jar of oil, yet through obedience to the prophet Elisha, she multiplied it to pay her debts and live off the rest.

"Then he said, Go, borrow thee vessels abroad of all thy neighbours, even empty vessels; borrow not a few." (2 Kings 4:3)

She increased her financial standing by using her limited resources with faith and secured her family's future.

2. **Joseph's Management in Egypt**
   Despite being sold into slavery, Joseph utilized his administrative gifts to rise to power in Egypt. His wise management during the years of plenty prepared the nation for famine, showcasing how his talents led to prosperity for himself and others.

"And he gathered up all the food of the seven years, which were in the land of Egypt, and laid up the food in the cities." (Genesis 41:48)

3. **The Fishermen Disciples**
   The disciples were seasoned fishermen, yet when Jesus called them, they began to follow Him. After an unsuccessful night of fishing, Jesus instructed them to cast their nets again, leading to a miraculous catch.

"And when they had this done, they enclosed a great multitude of fishes: and their net brake." (Luke 5:6)

By following Christ's instructions with their existing skills, they provided for their families and became fishers of men.

We position ourselves for divine provision when we step out in faith and utilize our God-given talents.

This promise is not just for material needs but encompasses all aspects of our lives.

Examples of Faith and Increase

1. **The Samaritan's Hospitality**
   In **Luke 10:25-37**, the Good Samaritan demonstrated compassion by using his resources to care for the wounded man. His actions reflected God's love and showcased how using what we have can impact lives.

"But a certain Samaritan, as he journeyed, came where he was: and when he saw him, he had compassion on him." (Luke 10:33)

2. **David's Skills as a Musician**
   Before becoming king, David used his musical talent to soothe King Saul's troubled spirit. This gave him a place in the king's court and paved the way for his future leadership.

"And it came to pass, when the evil spirit from God was upon Saul, that David took an harp, and played with his hand: so Saul was refreshed." (1 Samuel 16:23)

3. **Moses and His Staff**
   Moses initially doubted his ability to lead the Israelites out of Egypt. However, God instructed him to use what he had—his staff. With it, Moses performed miracles and led his people to freedom.

"And the Lord said unto him, What is that in thine hand? And he said, A rod." (Exodus 4:2)

The Importance of Using What You Have

The common thread in these examples is that each individual used their existing skills and resources to fulfill God's purpose. You don't need to invent something new; you need to activate what's already inside you. God doesn't call the equipped; He equips the called.

As you reflect on this chapter, consider your talents and gifts. Are you actively using them to increase your financial situation and support your family? Remember, God has placed you where you are for a reason, and He has given you the ability to create wealth and build a life that honors Him.

In this journey of increasing your money and utilizing your talents, trust in God's ability to multiply your efforts. Just as He took five loaves and two fish to feed the multitude, He can take what you have and make it more than enough. So step out in faith, use what you've been given, and watch God transform your life and finances in ways you never imagined.

Recognizing Your Talents

Recognizing your talents is crucial in building a fulfilling and prosperous life. Often, our gifts are hidden in plain sight, woven into our daily activities and interactions. Here are some key ways to identify and embrace your unique abilities.

1. Reflect on Your Passions

Think about the activities that energize you. What do you love to do in your free time? Your passions often reveal your talents. For example, if you enjoy creating art, you might have a talent for visual expression.

2. Consider Your Skills

List the skills you've developed personally and professionally over the years. This could include anything from communication skills to technical abilities. Ask yourself which skills you excel at and enjoy using.

3. Seek Feedback from Others

Sometimes, others see strengths in us that we might overlook. Ask friends, family, or colleagues what they think your talents are.

Their insights can help you recognize qualities you may not have considered.

4. Evaluate Your Accomplishments

Look back on your life and identify moments of achievement. What were you doing when you felt proud or accomplished? This reflection can highlight your natural talents and the contexts in which they shine.

5. Pay Attention to What Comes Naturally

Notice the tasks that seem more manageable for you compared to others. If you find yourself quickly grasping concepts or excelling in certain areas without much effort, those may be indicators of your innate talents.

6. Explore New Activities

Sometimes, stepping out of your comfort zone can help you discover hidden talents. Try new activities or hobbies and pay attention to what feels right and what you excel at. You might uncover a new passion or skill.

7. Assess Your Values

Your core values can also inform your talents. Consider what matters most to you in life. For instance, if you value helping others, you may have a talent for counseling or community service.

8. Look for Patterns in Your Life

Reflect on recurring themes or patterns in your life experiences. Do you consistently find yourself in leadership, creativity, or problem-solving roles? Recognizing these patterns can guide you toward your strengths.

9. Pray for Insight

Don't hesitate to ask God for guidance as you seek to uncover your talents. Pray for clarity and understanding of the gifts He has placed within you. Trust that He will reveal your purpose in His time.

10. Embrace Growth and Learning

Recognizing your talents is just the beginning. Be open to developing them further through education, practice, and experience. Commit to lifelong learning, enhancing your abilities, and opening new doors.

Biblical Examples of Recognizing Talents

1. **Moses**: Initially hesitant about his speaking ability, Moses eventually recognized his leadership potential when God called him to lead the Israelites out of Egypt. His staff became a symbol of his authority in guiding his people.

"And the Lord said unto him, What is that in thine hand? And he said, A rod." (Exodus 4:2)

2. **David**: A shepherd boy who recognized his talent for music and leadership, David used his skills to comfort King Saul and ultimately lead a nation.

"And David played with his hand, as at other times: and there was a javelin in Saul's hand." (1 Samuel 19:10)

3. **Esther**: Though initially unaware of her royal calling, Esther embraced her unique position and talents to save her people, demonstrating courage and strategic thinking.

"For if thou altogether holdest thy peace at this time, then shall there enlargement and deliverance arise to the Jews from another place." (Esther 4:14)

Recognizing your talents is an essential step in fulfilling your God-given purpose. By reflecting on your passions, seeking feedback, and exploring new avenues, you can uncover the gifts that God has placed within you. Embrace these talents and use them to impact your life and the lives of those around you. Remember, your unique abilities are not just for your benefit—they are part of a greater plan to serve your family and the Kingdom of God.

Courageous Confessions

1. **I recognize the value of my talents and will use them to increase my income.**

"For I know the thoughts that I think toward you, saith the Lord..." (Jeremiah 29:11 KJV)

2. **God has equipped me to succeed in my endeavors.**

"Thou shalt remember the Lord thy God: for it is he that giveth thee power to get wealth..." (Deuteronomy 8:18 KJV)

3. **I commit to developing my skills and investing in my growth.**

"The hand of the diligent shall bear rule: but the slothful shall be under tribute." (Proverbs 12:24 KJV)

4. **I am ready to take action and launch my ideas into reality.**

"Commit thy works unto the Lord, and thy thoughts shall be established." - Proverbs 16:3

5. **I will persevere through challenges because my effort will yield results.**

"And let us not be weary in well doing: for in due season we shall reap, if we faint not." (Galatians 6:9 KJV)

6. **I trust that God will multiply my efforts and bless my**

endeavors.

“And God is able to make all grace abound toward you; that ye, always having all sufficiency in all things, may abound to every good work.” (2 Corinthians 9:8 KJV)

7. I choose to be diligent and committed to my financial growth.

“The hand of the diligent maketh rich...” (Proverbs 10:4 KJV

8. I embrace the unique path God has set for me, knowing He equips me for every challenge.

"I will instruct thee and teach thee in the way which thou shalt go: I will guide thee with mine eye." - Psalm 32:8)

9. I am creating a legacy for my family through my actions today.

“A good man leaveth an inheritance to his children's children...” (Proverbs 13:22 KJV)

10. I will celebrate every small victory as I build my financial future.

“This is the day which the Lord hath made; we will rejoice and be glad in it.” (Psalm 118:24 KJV)

Track & Reflect

Complete Increase My Money in your Take Time to Build Companion Guide & Tracker

CHAPTER EIGHT: TAKE TIME TO B.U.I.L.D. FRAMEWORK

B - Believe in Your Gifts
Recognize and trust the talents God has given you. Have faith in your ability to make an impact with what you already possess.
Scripture: "For we are His workmanship, created in Christ Jesus unto good works..." (Ephesians 2:10 KJV)

U - Understand Your Value
Acknowledge the worth of your skills and how they can serve others. Identify the unique contribution you can make.
Scripture: "The king's business requireth haste." (1 Samuel 21:8 KJV)

I - Invest in Growth
Commit to developing your abilities. Take courses, seek mentorship, or practice regularly to enhance your talents.
Scripture: "Whatsoever thy hand findeth to do, do it with thy might..." (Ecclesiastes 9:10 KJV)

L - Launch into Action
Take the first step and start small. Don't wait for the perfect moment —act with what you have.
Scripture: "And he said unto them, This is the word of the Lord unto Zerubbabel, saying, Not by might, nor by power, but by my spirit..." (Zechariah 4:6 KJV)

D - Determine to Reap the Harvest

Stay committed and monitor your progress. Celebrate small victories and adjust your strategies as needed.
Scripture: "And let us not be weary in well doing: for in due season we shall reap, if we faint not." (Galatians 6:9 KJV)

Following the BUILD framework, you can transform your God-given talents into financial opportunities that uplift your life and serve others. Start your journey today, trusting that God will increase what you have!

Track & Reflect

Complete **Take Time to B.U.I.L.D. Framework** your Take Time to Build Companion Guide & Tracker

www.ingramcontent.com/pod-product-compliance
Ingram Content Group UK Ltd.
Pitfield, Milton Keynes, MK11 3LW, UK
UKHW021332070726
13610UKWH00011B/40

9 798989 230037